Dreams 2:22
Dream Journal

By Jake Bullard

Dreams 2:22 Dream Journal
© 2019 by Jake Bullard
www.dreams222.com
100X Publishing

ISBN: 978-1671306004

Cover design by Kimberly Stillwagon
www.visionsalesconsulting.com

Welcome to *Dream Journaling!*

We are in the greatest time in history where Holy Spirit is being poured out onto all flesh. We are dreaming more, having more visions and prophesying more now than at any other time in the past. This is why I created this dream journal. You now have a special place to record the amazing ways that God speaks His personalized words to you.

People ask me all the time, "Jake, how can I remember my dreams better?" Some people even say, "I don't really dream a lot, but I want to. What can I do to dream more?" My answer many times is, "Be a good steward of what He is giving you and write them down." If you want to dream more, ask Him to speak to you in your sleep and rest time, then be ready to see amazing and impossible things while you sleep.

Habakkuk 2:2 NIV says, "Then the Lord replied; 'Write down the revelation and make it plain on tablets so that the herald may run with it.'" Maybe this verse resonates with you and it's why you've decided to invest in your dream life. By writing down your dreams, visions and prophetic words soon after you've received them, you will be able to go back in time to remind yourself of what the Lord says about you and what He has planned for you. Writing down my dreams and the interpretations of them has helped me navigate the storms of life and to stand on the personal words and promises of God until they come into fruition. It has been a game changer for me, and I know it will be for you too.

How to Journal:

So, now that you have a journal to write your dreams and interpretations in, how do you write them down? Here's some advice that I give to those I train:

1) Give your dream a title.
Assigning it a title will help you identify the theme of what Holy Spirit is saying to you in your dream. It will also help you quickly recall the dream for when you go back to read it in the future.

2) Write the dream in chronological order.
God is a God of order and that goes for His dreams too. Many times, the timetable of God is laid out in the order of the dream. This method will also help you and others discern if the dream is a prophetic dream, soul dream, a "bad pizza" dream or a dream from the enemy. Realizing that a dream's sequence of events is important will help you hear Holy Spirit's interpretation and what His plans are for you or others.

3) No outside context!
A word of caution! Adding facts, ideas and details from regular life circumstances is a common thing I see others do when they tell their dreams. However, doing so may actually hinder getting the proper interpretation. I know the temptation is to bring in information that seems to help fill the gaps, but remember "...Don't interpretations belong to God?" (Genesis 40:8). When we bring in outside context, it muddies the water of our hearing and can distract us

from the dream, its details and other things Holy Spirit may be saying in the dream.

4) Be sure to write down each thing that stood out to you in the dream.

What stood out to you as something curious, important or odd? The vehicles, people you interact with or observe, colors, animals, etc.? The meaning of the symbols help reveal the mystery God is hiding in your dream. "It is the glory of God to conceal a thing: but the honor of Kings is to search out a matter" (Proverbs 25:2 KJV). These metaphorical symbols in the night are the modern-day version of the parables like Jesus told. Why? Because He is still teaching through pictures and stories today.

5) HAVE FUN!

Dreams are an amazing way that God talks to His children. They are just as unique as our fingerprints, DNA or retinal eye scan; one is never like another. To me, that is the amazing creativity of Jesus in our sleep and you should wake up with a smile on your face knowing that He is talking to YOU.

As you dream, I encourage you to write your dreams down and seek Holy Spirit for the interpretation. Dreams and interpretations of dreams are a fun treasure hunt and journey that God takes us on. So, if you are dreaming, ask Holy Spirit for the interpretation because "He is a rewarder of those who diligently seek Him" (Hebrews 11:6 NKJV). If you don't receive an interpretation on your dream, that's okay. Go ahead and write down your dream, and then set out to gain the interpretation. "It is the glory of God to conceal a matter, to search out a matter is the glory of kings" (Proverbs 25:2 NKJV).

Below you will find a great example of how to write out a dream. It's from someone who sent me their dream in 2018. Using this dream as an example of how to write your dreams will help you stay on track and will give you hope that God is really talking to you in your sleep.

Here is the dream:

"Meat in the Oven" from Michelle H.
I am at work at the safe house on the early morning shift (it's still dark out), and I go in the kitchen to start making breakfast for the ladies. I open the oven and there are all kinds of meats already cooking in the oven. There is literally meat everywhere in the oven...on baking sheets. I turn to the toaster oven and there is even meat in there. I begin asking the two ladies that are awake if they had placed it there and they said no, it was another lady in the house who had placed it there. So, I go to the manager's room to start cleaning it up, and as I go in the bathroom, I notice someone had already sprinkled Comet cleanser all over the bathroom. As I face the mirror over the sink, I look at myself and see something brown poking out my ear. I reach and pull it out...it is an earthworm. As I pull it out, I was like *well that is weird*. I look again and I see something else the same shape, only it is white this time. I begin to pull it out, and as I'm pulling, it's harder to get out. Then, there is a popping

noise and I see this worm had a base with flange-like feelers on the end, almost like an octopus bottom with lots of little legs. I'm like *wow! That feels so much better!* Then, my boss walks in asking me what all the comet is all over for. I begin to explain to her that it was already there and how I had just come in there to clean it up when I noticed something in my ear. Then I woke up.

Michelle did an amazing job writing this dream using the best-practices we discussed a few pages ago. The dream had a title, was written in order, there is no outside context added, she mentioned the details that stood out, and she had fun. This dream is one of my favorites, partly because of how well she wrote the dream out.

Writing the interpretation down is also very important. Doing this will help you go back to see what the Lord has said over you, your marriage, your business, community, family, and more. Sometimes dreams even help us get back on track to what God has called us to do. Here is the interpretation Holy Spirit gave me and Michelle's response.

Interpretation:

Hey, Michelle. Here is what I have for you on your dream. Please take what fits and what doesn't, put that on the shelf for now.

The Lord has so cherished His early morning time with you and your diligence in preparing with Him on your daily journey. You have taken the call on your life very seriously and the desire to lead others and give them substance is a great desire in your heart. Because of your discipline in preparation to lead those He's called you to, He will be giving you the solid, spiritual meals for others to feast upon. You will not be giving "milk" to them, but spiritual "meat" and "meat" that will never end. You will always have something great to give because of your season of preparation.

He's also cleaning out your ears of the earthly things that can clog up your spiritual ears. He's doing this so you can clearly hear how to feed the meat to others in a way they can chew on and digest with ease.

You have also been going through your own cleansing time where He has shown you small things that needed to get cleaned up a bit. Now that you have gone through your time of cleansing in His righteousness, it's your time to shine. You can shine because you know it's Him shining through you for His glory.

Be ready to step into a large leadership role. Don't let it intimidate you, as this is from the Lord and it has been your heart's desire since you were 13. He placed that in you, grew you and will now take you higher than you ever thought possible.

I keep hearing you say, "It's too good to be true" in an innocent way, because you can't believe it's finally here for you to walk in. It's not too good to be true; it is true.

Hope that helps and gives you some clarity. Let me know how this sits with you.

Her response:

Oh my, Jake...you have no idea (well, maybe you do LOL) how this blesses me and brings SOOO much clarity. The age 13 is so crazy that you picked that up. It's not chronological, but spiritual age. I had been walking with the Lord for about 13 years when the seeds for these desires really began to be planted. And yes, every time I catch glimpses, I actually tell the Lord, "That's too good to be true." Thank you so much for taking the time to pray over and steward the gift you have been given.

This dream is a perfect example of how Jesus still speaks to us in dreams and that Holy Spirit still gives the interpretations of dreams to us. When He drops dreams into our spirit, it can literally change our lives. For Michelle, He spoke into the desire of her heart (that He gave her). It confirmed what she had been wanting to do for a very long time. And I know that this dream and Holy Spirit's interpretation gave her a recharge in her heart to go after the dreams He gave her.

This dream is a great example of how to write your dream. But how do you break down a dream so that you can see what Holy Spirit is communicating to you (or to another dreamer who you are interpreting for)?

Glad you asked! My go-to is to always ask, "Holy Spirit, what are You saying in this dream?" In Genesis 40:8, Joseph says, "...do not interpretations belong to God? Tell me your dream." Having Holy Spirit living in you means you have all of Him and all of His gifts, including interpretation. So, as you are asking Him what the interpretation for the dream is, here is an outline for interpretation that can help you zero in to hear His voice more clearly.

1) Who is the dream about? Are you the focal point of the dream (living the dream in first person) or are you observing like a watching a movie?

2) What in the dream stands out the *most*? People, colors, animals, buildings, etc.

3) Are there any repeated themes in the dream? This could be the same color over and over or numbers that repeat themselves in the dream. If so, you will want to pay close attention to those things from the dream.

4) What is the mood of the dream?

5) Does the dream take place in the daytime or at night?

This outline is a good place to start so that you can begin to recognize what the Lord is saying to you and to others in their dreams. Once you have this down, remember to look at the symbols in the dream as metaphorical symbols. Dreams are a parable in the night. Use the Bible as your reference to those symbols and ask Holy Spirit for the interpretation, and you will start to see your dream life take off.

I hope this inspires you to dream, journal them and to seek out the interpretation. He loves to communicate with His creation, and He is communicating with you, even while you sleep.

Now your treasure hunt begins. Enjoy the journey.

May God bless your dreams,
—*Jake Bullard*

www.dreams222.com

Dream Title: _____
Date: _____

_____
_____
_____
_____
_____
_____
_____
_____
_____
_____
_____
_____
_____
_____
_____
_____
_____
_____
_____
_____
_____
_____
_____

Interpretation for Dream Title:

Date: _____

Dream Title: _____

Date: _____

Interpretation for Dream Title:

_____

Date: _____

_____

_____

_____

_____

_____

_____

_____

_____

_____

_____

_____

_____

_____

_____

_____

_____

_____

_____

_____

_____

_____

Dream Title: _____

Date: _____

Interpretation for Dream Title:

_____

Date: _____

_____
_____
_____
_____
_____
_____
_____
_____
_____
_____
_____
_____
_____
_____
_____
_____
_____
_____
_____
_____
_____
_____
_____

Dream Title: _____

Date: _____

_____

_____
_____
_____
_____
_____
_____
_____
_____
_____
_____
_____
_____
_____
_____
_____
_____
_____
_____
_____
_____
_____
_____
_____
_____
_____

Interpretation for Dream Title:

Date: _____

Dream Title: _____
Date: _____

_____
_____
_____
_____
_____
_____
_____
_____
_____
_____
_____
_____
_____
_____
_____
_____
_____
_____
_____
_____
_____
_____
_____
_____
_____
_____

Interpretation for Dream Title:

Date: _____

Dream Title: _____

Date: _____

_____
_____
_____
_____
_____
_____
_____
_____
_____
_____
_____
_____
_____
_____
_____
_____
_____
_____
_____
_____
_____
_____
_____
_____
_____

Interpretation for Dream Title:

_____

Date: _____

_____

_____
_____
_____
_____
_____
_____
_____
_____
_____
_____
_____
_____
_____
_____
_____
_____
_____
_____
_____
_____

Dream Title: _____

Date: _____

_____
_____
_____
_____
_____
_____
_____
_____
_____
_____
_____
_____
_____
_____
_____
_____
_____
_____
_____
_____
_____
_____
_____
_____
_____
_____

Interpretation for Dream Title:

_____

Date: _____

_____
_____
_____
_____
_____
_____
_____
_____
_____
_____
_____
_____
_____
_____
_____
_____
_____
_____
_____
_____
_____
_____
_____

Dream Title: _____

Date: _____

_____
_____
_____
_____
_____
_____
_____
_____
_____
_____
_____
_____
_____
_____
_____
_____
_____
_____
_____
_____
_____
_____
_____
_____
_____
_____
_____

Interpretation for Dream Title:

_____

Date: _____

_____
_____
_____
_____
_____
_____
_____
_____
_____
_____
_____
_____
_____
_____
_____
_____
_____
_____
_____
_____
_____
_____
_____

Dream Title: _____
Date: _____

Interpretation for Dream Title:

_____

Date: _____

Dream Title: _____

Date: _____

Interpretation for Dream Title:

_____

Date: _____

_____
_____
_____
_____
_____
_____
_____
_____
_____
_____
_____
_____
_____
_____
_____
_____
_____
_____
_____
_____
_____
_____

Dream Title: _____
Date: _____

Interpretation for Dream Title:

_____

Date: _____

_____
_____
_____
_____
_____
_____
_____
_____
_____
_____
_____
_____
_____
_____
_____
_____
_____
_____
_____
_____
_____
_____

Dream Title: _____

Date: _____

_____
_____
_____
_____
_____
_____
_____
_____
_____
_____
_____
_____
_____
_____
_____
_____
_____
_____
_____
_____
_____
_____
_____
_____
_____

Interpretation for Dream Title:

Date: _____

Dream Title: _____
Date: _____

_____
_____
_____
_____
_____
_____
_____
_____
_____
_____
_____
_____
_____
_____
_____
_____
_____
_____
_____
_____
_____
_____
_____
_____

Interpretation for Dream Title:

_____

Date: _____

_____
_____
_____
_____
_____
_____
_____
_____
_____
_____
_____
_____
_____
_____
_____
_____
_____
_____
_____
_____
_____

Dream Title: _____

Date: _____

Interpretation for Dream Title:

Date: _____

_____
_____
_____
_____
_____
_____
_____
_____
_____
_____
_____
_____
_____
_____
_____
_____
_____
_____
_____
_____
_____
_____
_____
_____
_____

Dream Title: _____

Date: _____

Interpretation for Dream Title:

Date: _____

_____

_____
_____
_____
_____
_____
_____
_____
_____
_____
_____
_____
_____
_____
_____
_____
_____
_____
_____
_____
_____
_____
_____

Dream Title: _____

Date: _____

Interpretation for Dream Title:

_____

Date: _____

❦

_____
_____
_____
_____
_____
_____
_____
_____
_____
_____
_____
_____
_____
_____
_____
_____
_____
_____
_____
_____
_____
_____
_____

Dream Title: _____

Date: _____

Interpretation for Dream Title:

_____

Date: _____

_____
_____
_____
_____
_____
_____
_____
_____
_____
_____
_____
_____
_____
_____
_____
_____
_____
_____
_____
_____

Dream Title: _____
Date: _____

_____
_____
_____
_____
_____
_____
_____
_____
_____
_____
_____
_____
_____
_____
_____
_____
_____
_____
_____
_____
_____
_____
_____
_____
_____

Interpretation for Dream Title:

Date: _____

_____
_____
_____
_____
_____
_____
_____
_____
_____
_____
_____
_____
_____
_____
_____
_____
_____
_____
_____
_____
_____
_____
_____

Dream Title: _____

Date: _____

Interpretation for Dream Title:

_____

Date: _____

_____

_____

_____

_____

_____

_____

_____

_____

_____

_____

_____

_____

_____

_____

_____

_____

_____

_____

_____

_____

_____

Dream Title: _____

Date: _____

———————————————————————————————

———————————————————————————————

———————————————————————————————

———————————————————————————————

———————————————————————————————

———————————————————————————————

———————————————————————————————

———————————————————————————————

———————————————————————————————

———————————————————————————————

———————————————————————————————

———————————————————————————————

———————————————————————————————

———————————————————————————————

———————————————————————————————

———————————————————————————————

———————————————————————————————

———————————————————————————————

———————————————————————————————

———————————————————————————————

———————————————————————————————

———————————————————————————————

———————————————————————————————

Interpretation for Dream Title:

_____

Date: _____

_____

_____

_____

_____

_____

_____

_____

_____

_____

_____

_____

_____

_____

_____

_____

_____

_____

_____

_____

_____

_____

_____

_____

_____

_____

Dream Title: _____

Date: _____

_____

_____

_____

_____

_____

_____

_____

_____

_____

_____

_____

_____

_____

_____

_____

_____

_____

_____

_____

_____

_____

_____

_____

_____

Interpretation for Dream Title:

Date: _____

Dream Title: _____
Date: _____

- - -

_____
_____
_____
_____
_____
_____
_____
_____
_____
_____
_____
_____
_____
_____
_____
_____
_____
_____
_____
_____
_____
_____
_____
_____
_____
_____
_____
_____

Interpretation for Dream Title:

Date: _____

Dream Title: _____

Date: _____

_____

_____
_____
_____
_____
_____
_____
_____
_____
_____
_____
_____
_____
_____
_____
_____
_____
_____
_____
_____
_____
_____
_____
_____
_____

Interpretation for Dream Title:

_____

Date: _____

Dream Title: _____
Date: _____

Interpretation for Dream Title:

_____

Date: _____

_____
_____
_____
_____
_____
_____
_____
_____
_____
_____
_____
_____
_____
_____
_____
_____
_____
_____
_____
_____
_____
_____
_____
_____

Author Bio:

Jake Bullard is a prophetic voice gifted with dream interpretations, words of knowledge and prophetic messages. He has a passion to see the body of Christ live in the awareness of their God-given identity and to walk in the fullness of knowing who they are in Christ and who He is in them. Jake also carries a unique ability to teach, train and equip others in the prophetic, especially with dream interpretations. He and his wife, Rachel, serve at Seven Springs Church in Powder Springs, GA, in several capacities.

The Dreams 2:22 community was created by Jake to give believers a place to post their dreams so that they may receive healthy interpretations to their dreams. Here, Jake also offers training courses so others may grow in understanding dreams and interpretations and how God uses them still today to speak to people all across the world. You can also schedule a dream consultation with Jake or one of his team members to discuss the details of your dream, the interpretation and the application of what Holy Spirit is saying to you.

Contact Jake Bullard at
knowingdreams222@gmail.com
or follow him on his Facebook fan page and group at
Dreams 2:22 to see his current offers.

www.dreams222.com

Made in the USA
Lexington, KY
14 December 2019